MEDITATIONS
FOR
CATS

FAVORITE FELINE PHILOSOPHIES

**PHOTOGRAPHS
BY ANNE HERMAN**

**Andrews McMeel
Publishing**

Kansas City

The secret to flying is
to throw yourself at the ground
and miss.

—*Douglas Adams*

Of all the things you wear,

your expression is the most important.

—*Janet Lane*

Underneath this flabby exterior
is an enormous lack of character.

—*Oscar Levant*

To sit in the shade on a fine day,

and look upon verdure

is the most perfect refreshment.

—*Jane Austen*

No one worth possessing

Can be quite possessed.

—*Sara Teasdale*

I don't care what anybody says about me
as long as it isn't true.

—*Dorothy Parker*

I go to seek the great Perhaps.

—*François Rabelais*

Dare to be naive.

—*Richard Buckminster Fuller*

Grub first, then ethics.

—*Bertolt Brecht*

What is more agreeable

than one's home?

—*Marcus Tullius Cicero*

There is less in this than meets the eye.

—*Tallulah Bankhead*

Remember, Ginger Rogers did
everything Fred Astaire did,
but she did it backwards and in high heels.

—*Faith Whittlesey*

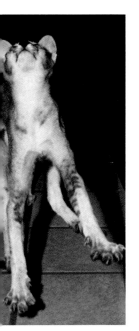
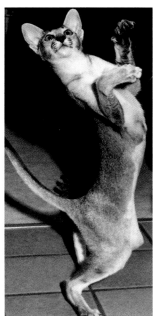
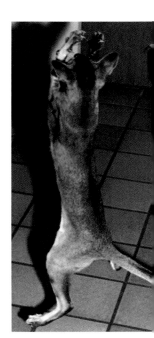

Ask yourself, What is this thing in itself,

by its own special constitution?

What is it in substance, and in form, and in matter?

What is its function in the world?

For how long does it subsist?

—*Marcus Aurelius*

When the lion sleeps,

don't wake him.

—*Yiddish saying*

If you are not too long,

I will wait here for you all my life.

—*Oscar Wilde*

An object in possession
seldom retains the same charm
that it had in pursuit.

—*Pliny the Younger*

A child of five would understand this.
Send somebody to fetch a child of five!

—*Groucho Marx in* Duck Soup

Whatever else is unsure

in this stinking dunghill of a world

a mother's love is not.

—*James Joyce*

You'll come to learn a great deal
if you study the insignificant in depth.

—*Odysseus Elytis*

To knock a thing down,

especially if it is cocked at an arrogant angle,

is a deep delight to the blood.

—*George Santayana*

I am not the type

who wants to go back to the land;

I am the type who wants to go back to the hotel.

—*Fran Lebowitz*

Who can refute a sneer?

—*William Paley*

Neurosis is always a substitute
for legitimate suffering.

—*Carl Jung*

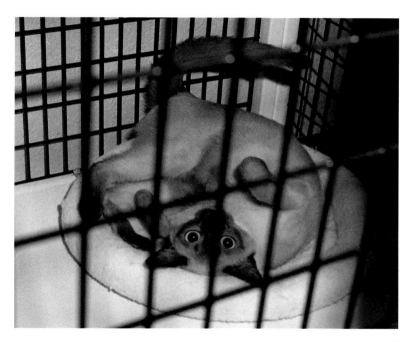

Alone bad. Friend good.

Friend good!

—*Monster (Boris Karloff)*
in The Bride of Frankenstein

But we're such little creatures . . . so fragile, so weak.

Little . . . little animals.

—*Edward Chapman (Pippa/Raymond Passworthy)*

to Raymond Massey (John/Oswald Cabal)

in Things to Come

You must learn to be still in the midst of activity

and to be vibrantly alive in repose.

—Indira Gandhi

Nothing gives one so much advantage over another

as to remain always cool and unruffled

under all circumstances.

—*Thomas Jefferson*

Everything tries to be round.

—*Black Elk*

The kiss you take is better than you give.

—*William Shakespeare*

The worst sin—

perhaps the only sin—passion can commit,

is to be joyless.

—*Dorothy Leigh Sayers*

I have always been able to gain my living
without doing any work.

—*Mark Twain*

It is completely unimportant.

That is why it is so interesting.

—*Agatha Christie*

See the happy moron,

he doesn't give a damn.

I wish I were a moron—

My God, perhaps I am!

—Anonymous

Do not eat before you have fed your animal.

—*Talmud*

It was such a lovely day

I thought it was a pity to get up.

—*Somerset Maugham*

Bloom where you are planted.

—*Anonymous*

Architecture will be soft and hairy.

—*Antonio Gaudí*

Pleasure is the beginning

and the end of living happily.

—*Epicurus*

I have often wished I had time

to cultivate modesty...

But I am too busy thinking about myself.

—*Dame Edith Sitwell*

Meditations for Cats © 2000 Watershed Books, LLC.
Photographs © Anne Herman.

ISBN: 0-7407-1463-5

Library of Congress Catalog Card Number: 00-106945